"The Concept2 RowErg is used by people of all ages and abilities who want a full-body, low-impact workout. Whether you're just starting out on your fitness journey, looking to start something new, or a long-time athlete, learning proper technique will help you row better and faster in the long run."

ALEX DUNNE, MANAGING DIRECTOR, CONCEPT2 LTD

"The indoor rowing machine is one of the most fantastic and easy ways to get into the sport of rowing for the first time, as well as a great tool to help people keep fit and complement on-water rowing. It offers a low-impact cardio workout that uses 85% of your muscles and 9 major muscle groups. Both indoor and on-water rowing are also brilliant ways to socialise with others through online and in-person communities. They are both also excellent forms of exercise to improve your mental health — whether you row on real water, race against others, or online in virtual worlds."

CHRIS FARRELL, NATIONAL PROJECT MANAGER FOR INDOOR ROWING, BRITISH ROWING

INDOOR ROWING MASTERY:

Unlocking Your Potential

By Multiple World Record Holder

CAT TRENTHAM

CONTENTS

INTRODUCTION

Thank you for buying my book!

Whether you're a complete beginner or an experienced rower looking to take your skills to the next level, this book provides comprehensive instruction and guidance to master the indoor rowing machine. I've written this book as I know how much I would have loved to have had access to this resource when I was first starting! I hope you will find it both educational and helpful.

MY STORY

At the age of 29, I let my friend Andy talk me into entering an indoor rowing competition. I was no stranger to the machine: I'd been using it for warm-ups and workouts since I started going to the gym at age 14, but I was no expert.

My race was a 500m sprint at the English Indoor Championships. Naturally, I thought the best way to train for this was to practice max-effort 500m pieces repeatedly! It was not. But I did well - very well. When I stopped comparing my scores to those of my male counterparts and started comparing them to scores of other lightweight ladies in my age group, I realised: Wow, I'm actually pretty good at this! In my first-ever competition, and after four weeks of training, I had done enough to earn a bronze medal.

By this point, I had caught the bug. My technique was terrible, literally awful! I was relying on brute strength and determination alone! Learning to clean this up and become more efficient allowed me to pull much better scores without additional effort. Everything felt better and more controlled.

By the time I went to my next competition a few months later, I had two British records under my belt and won gold on the day. I was unstoppable.

From here, I hired a fantastic coach, Casey, who programmed my workouts. I achieved more British records, World records, and numerous medals. I also began rowing on water (mostly sculling, but sweep rowing too). My success in the boat never matched my success on the erg, but it taught me many important lessons about improving rowing proficiency. My background in indoor and on-water rowing has allowed me to take the best aspects of both training modalities, alongside my knowledge of what it takes to become a champion and use these to become the best rowing coach I can be.

I advise aspiring rowers to improve their technique and invest in excellent programming. These things will take you from good to great and allow efficiency to work in your favour.

Please visit cattrenthampersonaltraining.com for details of my indoor rowing programmes and coaching services.

THE ANATOMY OF A CONCEPT2 ROWING MACHINE

Many rowing machine brands can be found on the market, but this book will focus on the Concept2 rowing machine. Concept2 is renowned for its use in official competitions and is widely acknowledged as the industry benchmark.

Let's explore the structure and components of the machine:

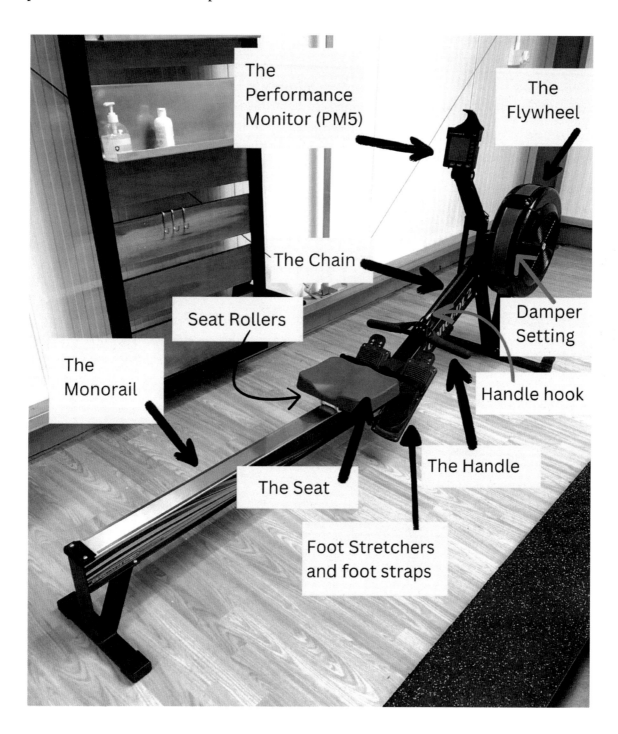

SETTING UP THE ROWING MACHINE

DRAG FACTOR

Contrary to popular belief, how hard you pull the handle rather than the damper setting determines the difficulty level when using the indoor rowing machine.

Changing the damper or drag alters the amount of air passing through the flywheel. It is always better to set your machine up using drag factor rather than just guessing a "level" to put it on, as level 10 on one erg may feel like a level 4 on another. Depending on factors like age and if the fan needs cleaning, there can be much variance between machines.

For an optimal workout and to minimise the risk of injury, it is crucial to maintain an appropriate drag factor when rowing. If the drag factor is too high, it can cause excessive strain on the body and increase the risk of injury. On the other hand, if the drag factor is too low, the workout may not provide enough resistance to challenge the body and achieve the desired results.

For the most part, I typically recommend a drag factor of 115-125 for women and 130-135 for men for most workouts (with lighter athletes generally opting for the lower end of each range). However, for short sprints, the drag factor can be increased by 10.

HOW TO SET YOUR DRAG FACTOR

Select 'More Options' on the monitor and then 'Display Drag Factor'. Row a few strokes until a number appears in the box. Move the damper higher or lower to increase or decrease the drag until the desired number is displayed. (You can view the drag factor on apps such as ErgData without the need to navigate through the menu).

OPTIMISING FOOT POSITION

Optimal foot height will allow your shins to become (but not exceed) vertical at the front end (catch position), enabling a good range of motion and putting you in a solid position to generate maximum power. The optimal height for your feet will depend on several factors, such as height, shin length and flexibility in your lower legs.

HOW TO DETERMINE FOOT POSITION

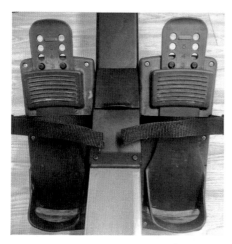

Move the foot stretchers up or down to find your optimal foot height.

Shins should be vertical at the catch so you can generate as much power as possible.

If your feet are too low, you are in a weaker position, making your next stroke harder than it needs to be. The shins have exceeded the vertical position.

If your feet are too high, you will lose power due to a reduced range of motion. Your shins need to become more vertical.

MAKING THE SEAT MORE COMFORTABLE

Comfort on an indoor rowing machine seat is crucial. Optimal comfort enhances focus during workouts by minimising distractions and therefore boosting overall performance. Motivation and consistency will likely increase when discomfort is eliminated, even during extended sessions.

Feeling uncomfortable on the seat for extended periods may result in poor posture and added stress on the lower back, hips, and pelvis. Over time, this can lead to discomfort, pain, and potential injury. To prevent these issues, consider investing in a seat pad. The Concept2 online shop is an excellent place for purchasing these pads, which offer added comfort during longer rows and prevent slipping during shorter rows or sprints. They are a valuable accessory for any rowing workout.

Alternatively, a folded towel can be placed on the seat for comfort. Ensure the towel doesn't overhang as it could get caught in the monorail during exercise.

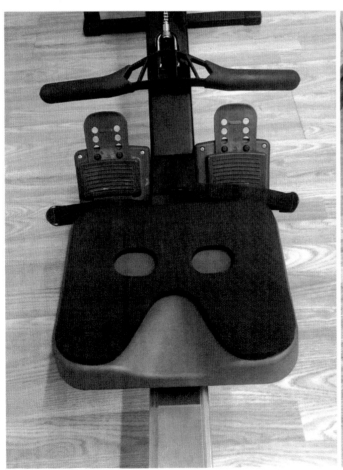

BEST FOOTWEAR

Choosing the correct footwear is essential for indoor rowing as it affects power transmission. Adidas Powerlift shoes are my preferred choice due to their flat sole, which enables a good footplate connection, and their lower heel height and flexible toe, which allow for a full range of motion. This combination promotes efficient power transmission and optimal performance during rowing workouts.

Other Olympic lifting shoes also provide a solid footplate connection, but their larger heel heights or inflexible toes may slightly restrict the range of motion. To compensate for this, you can adjust the height of the foot stretchers. Alternatively, regular trainers provide an excellent range of motion, but they may not offer the same level of footplate connection as lifting shoes.

On-water rowers who use the erg often row in only socks or barefoot to replicate the sensation of being in a boat, to minimise foot movement, and to enhance their awareness of weight distribution at the catch position. Choosing the correct footwear can provide similar benefits to barefoot rowing while allowing users to secure their feet and prevent potential irritation to the tops of their feet from the straps.

PROTECTING YOUR HANDS

HOW TO HOLD THE HANDLE CORRECTLY

For the best handle grip, hold it in the curve of your fingers with an overhand grip, placing your hands towards the outer edges. To avoid wrist strain and enhance efficiency, keep your wrists flat.

Avoid the temptation to hold the handle in your palms. Your grip should be relaxed and secure, which will help minimise blisters and ensure proper grip position for effective power transmission throughout the rowing stroke.

Fingerless weight-lifting gloves will be of little use in rowing as they won't extend to the curve of the fingertips and will not provide cushioning in the correct place.

Flat wrists ✓
Hands to the outer edges of the handle ✓
Handle in the curve of fingertips ✓

Wrists are bent ✗
Hands too close together ✗
The handle is in the palms of the hands ✗

DEALING WITH BLISTERS

It is not unusual for people who row regularly to experience some soreness and blistering on their fingers from time to time due to holding the handle for extended periods. Usually, this occurs in people covering large distances on the machine or in people who increase their volume too quickly before their hands have had a chance to adapt appropriately. Over time, this should be fine.

If sore fingers are making it difficult for you to complete your next row, kinesiology tape wrapped around the sore point can provide some added protection. Although not its traditional use (its primary purposes are supporting and reducing swelling in painful muscles and joints), it tends to be a great option as it is waterproof, so it shouldn't come off even if you get sweaty. It is also much more flexible than a regular plaster, allowing for good mobility through the fingers.

I like the ready-cut finger tape from the company WODnDONE. Still, you can easily make your own by buying a regular roll of kinesiology tape (from Amazon, Boots etc.) and cutting it down into finger-sized pieces.

If you have an open wound or blister, place a small piece of lint-free dressing on top of it before applying the tape; this will help keep it clean, stop the tape from sticking directly to it, and provide an additional layer of padding. Upon completing your row, you should remove the tape, clean the area, apply something like Savlon and then keep it uncovered to allow the air to get to it as much as possible. Savlon will serve as an antiseptic, keep the skin supple and help it to heal. (For any nasty blisters, it is usually best to avoid rowing altogether to allow your skin time to heal.)

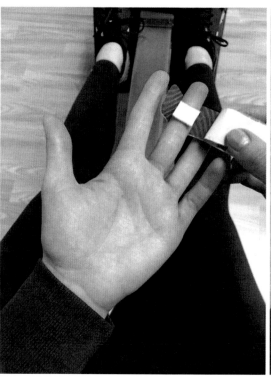

TECHNIQUE AND SEQUENCING

Improving your rowing technique takes time and consistent practice, but the rewards are worth the effort: it is the fastest route to achieving better scores! Improving your technical ability can lead to better utilisation of your strength, resulting in a higher power output. In addition, a superior technique will minimise energy waste and increase endurance, allowing you to maintain a higher work rate for longer durations.

There are four different parts to the rowing stroke:

- **The Catch:** Your start position at the front of the machine.
- **The Drive Phase:** The movement from the catch to the finish. (This is where all the power happens!)
- **The Finish:** Your position at the back end of the machine.
- **The Recovery Phase:** The movement from the finish back to the catch.

Let's take a look at how you can improve the specifics of each:

THE CATCH

- Sit tall with a straight back. Shoulders should be relaxed.

- You should have an overhand grip, with hands spaced evenly apart at the outer edges of the handle. Wrists should be flat.

- Your body should be hinged forwards (through the hips, not the back). Your body will be compressed against your thighs.

- Notice how the shins are vertical but do not exceed vertical.

- If you are in the correct position, a gap will be visible between the front of the seat and your ankles; this should be the case every time you return to the catch position. If your seat hits your ankles, you should be hinged forwards more.

THE DRIVE PHASE

- Begin in the catch position.
- Body hinged forwards, weight through the feet.

- Push hard through your legs whilst keeping your arms straight. This part of the movement is like that performed on a leg press machine.
- The legs are the main driving force of the movement and are where the majority of your power will come from. For this reason, rowing should be considered more of a pushing action than pulling.

- Upon the legs straightening, lean back with your body to engage power through your hips and back.

- Finish by pulling the arms to your lower chest. (About level with the bottom of your sports bra for women). Don't allow your elbows to flare too wide.
- The chain should be level and maintain a straight line throughout the stroke.
- You are now at the finish position.

THE FINISH

- Legs should be straight, and the chain should be level and pulled to the lower chest.

- Wrists should still be flat, with your hands on the outer edges of the handle.

- You will be rocked back from the hips.

- Despite being hinged backwards, you should still be sat tall with a straight back. Always try to elongate yourself as much as possible.

- Shoulders should be relaxed, and elbows shouldn't be flared too wide.

THE RECOVERY PHASE

- Similar to the drive phase, but in reverse.

- The recovery phase is often completed more slowly than the drive phase (especially at low stroke rates). The drive phase is explosive, whereas the recovery is precisely that: a recovery to prepare yourself for the effort of the next stroke. Smooth and steady is key.

- You will begin the recovery phase from the finish position.

- Straighten your arms out. For now, your legs should stay straight, and your body should still be rocked backwards.

- Once the arms are straight, allow the body to rock forwards.

- Hinge from your hips rather than your back as you do this.

- The handle should be forwards of the knees.

- Ensure you stay in control of the movement and you don't allow the chain to pull you back in.

- Continue to sit tall as you bend the legs and slide back up the rail.

- The chain should move in a straight line throughout.

- Allow the heels to lift at the very front.

- You are now back at the catch position, ready to begin another stroke.

With practice, the stroke should become smoother and much more fluid.

An excellent way to assess your technique is to film yourself from the side: Is your back straight? Are you pushing with the legs? Is the sequencing right? What still needs work?

Use the steady sessions in your programme to concentrate on practising good technique.

For additional help with your indoor rowing technique, visit cattrenthampersonaltraining.com for details of my coaching services.

WARM-UPS AND COOL-DOWNS

With an understanding of the rowing mechanics in place, let's explore how to structure sessions, starting with the warm-up.

For most sessions, it is a good idea to do a warm-up and a cool-down on either end.

Low-intensity, steady sessions do not require warm-ups and cool-downs, but you can do a short one if desired.

Warm-Ups should be a moderate effort. They are an excellent opportunity to practice the technique and prepare your body (and mind) ahead of a tough session. Warm-ups become even more important as the session's intensity increases. Properly warming up your muscles will help prevent injuries when performing something like max-effort sprints.

An example of a warm-up is 1000m at a moderate pace.
If the workout ahead includes short sprints, add 1 or 2 short bursts (of 50-100m) at the end of your 1000m moderate effort, performed at a much faster pace to help further prepare you for your session.

Give yourself 2-4 minutes between completing your warm-up and beginning your workout to allow your heart rate and breathing to settle and to give your mind a moment of calm.

Cool-Downs should be performed slowly and with little effort. They are great for helping flush out some of the lactic acid accumulated during the session and slowly return your heart rate to normal.

An example of a cool down is 500-1000m at a very gentle effort.

A NOTE ON FLEXIBILITY

If hamstring flexibility limits your range of motion during the recovery phase, you can add some stretches to your warm-up. Do this following your initial warm-up on the rowing machine. (If your range of motion is already good, there is no need to do this.)

Sit on the floor with your legs straight and feet flexed, and reach for your toes. Do this gently and be careful not to force a position which feels too uncomfortable. You do not need to touch your toes; just aim to reach a point where you can feel a stretch in your hamstrings, the muscles located on the backs of your thighs. Perform this 3-4 times, for roughly 10 seconds each time. Add this into your warm-up on each rowing session for as long as needed. Over time your hamstring flexibility should gradually increase, allowing you to obtain a fuller range of movement at the catch position.

TYPES OF WORKOUT

To maximise your rowing performance, you must include diverse workouts targeting various energy systems within your body. By addressing all aspects of training, you can lay a solid foundation that enables specialisation when required for optimal results. Let's take a look at what these are:

- **Steady State (SS):** These workouts are usually long in length and low in intensity. These continuous endurance training pieces (sometimes called base training) use the **aerobic energy system** (meaning your muscles are using a constant supply of oxygen). They can be enjoyable and are usually only moderately taxing. An example of a long steady-state workout in indoor rowing could be a 60-minute row with a cap of 18 strokes per minute.

- **High-Intensity Interval Training (HIIT):** Repeated high-intensity work intervals with rests. These are usually short bursts of work at a near-maximal effort, mainly using the **anaerobic energy system** (whereby the body breaks down glucose without oxygen). These workouts are very taxing and produce lactic acid as a bi-product, which will cause a burning sensation in the muscles. An example of a rowing HIIT workout could be 10 x 100m with 1.30 rests.

- **Intervals (a mix of SS and HIIT):** You can also do longer intervals, which use more of a combination of aerobic and anaerobic energy systems. These are intense workouts, but much longer than anything that could be performed at maximum intensity. An example might be 6 x 750m with 2.30 rests.

- **Sprints:** Sprints will always predominantly use an anaerobic energy system, similar to HIIT. However, if the workout is a test piece with the aim of a personal best, longer rests between attempts may be required to achieve a fuller recovery between efforts. This recovery period might be based on a perception of recovery rather than a set time to qualify for an all-out maximal effort every time. For example, when attempting your best 100m score, your workout (following an adequate warm-up) might consist of 3-4 attempts of 100m, with rests as long as needed in between.

TYPES OF WORKOUT ON THE ROWING MACHINE

Now that we're familiar with various training methods, let us examine how the rowing machine offers options for building your workouts and identify which methods mentioned earlier may align best with each approach.

- **Just Row:** The most basic workout mode, where all numbers begin at zero and count up (time and distance) as soon as you commence rowing. Avoid resting for extended periods during a "Just Row" workout, as the monitor will turn itself off after inactivity of around two to three minutes (or sooner if the batteries are low). To prevent this, press either the "Units" or "Display" button and cycle back to your preference. Avoid pressing the "Menu" button before finishing your workout, as this will end it!

- **Single Distance:** A set distance, programmed into the monitor and completed once. The monitor will show the number of meters awaiting completion. They will count down as you row. Examples of a single-distance workout could be 500m, 2000m, or 10,000m.

- **Single Time:** A set time, programmed into the monitor and completed once. The time is programmed into the monitor and will count down once you begin the row. Examples of a single-time workout could be 1 minute, 30 minutes or 60 minutes.

- **Single Calorie:** A set number of calories is inputted into the monitor and completed once. The monitor will display the number of remaining calories which will reduce as you continue to row. This book and the programmes on my website do not focus on calorie-based rowing sessions; the focuses are on times and distances. But in essence, when rowing for calories, a more strenuous effort (faster split time) will result in the number of calories being satisfied more quickly.

- **Intervals:** Interval sessions are a type of workout that involves completing multiple repetitions. During these sessions, you take rests in between each repetition. There are two types of interval sessions: constant intervals and variable intervals, which are explained below.

- **Constant Intervals:** Constant intervals are characterised by the same work and rest periods for each repetition, creating a consistent pattern throughout the workout. For example, a distance-interval session might involve 8 repetitions of 500m with 2 minutes of rest between each repetition. A time-interval session could include 15 repetitions of 1 minute, with 1 minute of rest in between. Likewise, a calorie-interval session might consist of 10 repetitions of 20 calories, with 45 seconds of rest between each repetition.

- **Variable Intervals:** Variable intervals involve completing repetitions where the work and rest time vary, creating a changing pattern throughout the workout. For instance, a variable interval session could consist of 1000 meters of work followed by 2.30 minutes of rest, 750 meters of work followed by 2.00 minutes of rest, 500 meters of work followed by 1.30 minutes of rest, and 250 meters of work with one minute of rest.

A NOTE ON INTERVAL SESSIONS

For optimal performance during interval sessions, beginning each repetition from a static start is recommended. This means waiting until the rest period ends and the new repetition is visible on the screen before rowing. This practice can improve the continuity of your scores and increase your power through the first few strokes.

To avoid negatively affecting your split time, refrain from picking up the handle until you are ready to start the first repetition, as unintentional movements may trigger the monitor to begin clocking the workout earlier than intended, harming your score. On subsequent repetitions, ensure you are ready to begin as soon as it is time to start, as delays can impact your split time and not reflect your true capabilities.

During interval workouts, you can either rest entirely or keep moving gently during the rest period. My preference would always be for complete rest. Sit still and quiet, and take a sip of water if necessary. Concentrate on bringing your breathing rate down and mentally preparing yourself for the effort of your next repetition.

HOW WORKOUTS ARE WRITTEN

Now that we've reviewed the components of a workout, it's helpful to explore how these may be presented in written form. This is relevant as this is how you will encounter them in structured rowing programmes. Following a programme tailored to your needs is highly recommended to help you achieve your goals. Arriving at the gym and deciding on a workout spontaneously does not typically align with obtaining the best results!

When rowing workouts are written, they are often written in a simplified format. They are written as the work to be completed, followed by details on the stroke rate they should be performed at. If no stroke rate is advised, you should assume it is a free rate piece (i.e. no specified stroke rate). An interval workout will include the number of repetitions and the duration of rest periods.

Note that the following abbreviations can be expected:

" Seconds

' Minutes

r (if in front of a number, this refers to the stroke rate. If it follows a number, this relates to the rest period).

Here are some examples:

8 x 250m / 90"r is a constant distance interval workout. Each time, the distance to be completed is 250 meters; the rest period is 90 seconds. Eight repetitions should be completed.

15 x 1' / 1'r is a constant time interval workout. Each time the work period and rest period are both 1 minute. Fifteen repetitions should be completed.

50' @ r18/r19/r20/r21/r22 is a single-time workout of 50 minutes, with five stroke rate changes. Unless otherwise specified, you should assume that each stroke rate section is of equal length. (In this example: 10 minutes). The first section should be performed at 18 strokes per minute, followed by the second section at 19 strokes per minute, and so on, with the final section at 22 strokes per minute.

2000m is a single-distance workout. No stroke rate is provided, so we can assume it is a free rate piece.

1000m-750m-500m-250m. Rests are 1.30' is a variable interval workout. The first interval is 1000m, then there is a rest of 1 minute and 30 seconds. The following interval is 750m, then there is a 1 minute 30 rest, and so on.

THE INTENSITY OF WORKOUTS

To optimise your training and achieve your fitness goals, it is important to have a clear divide between high-intensity, moderate-intensity, and low-intensity sessions. Each type of session serves a unique purpose in your training regimen.

High-intensity workouts are ideal for testing your limits, measuring improvement, and pushing yourself to achieve fast split times. While these sessions are crucial for improving performance, your body cannot handle them all the time.

Additional training volume at lower intensities is necessary to improve high-intensity workouts. This volume can be achieved through moderate-intensity sessions, which are challenging but not a maximal effort, and low-intensity sessions, which are steady-state and help to increase your aerobic base.

Low-intensity work is especially important for improving your aerobic capacity, delivering oxygen to your muscles, and building muscular endurance. This, in turn, allows you to complete more work and recover more quickly, leading to improvements in top-end, high-intensity workouts. Lower-intensity sessions also provide an opportunity to improve your technique and power per stroke.

It is important to avoid pushing too hard during low-intensity sessions. Doing so can prevent essential adaptations from occurring and dilute your performance during high-intensity sessions due to inadequate recovery.

HEART RATE WORKOUT ZONES

Heart rate training is a technique that utilises heart rate as an indicator of exercise intensity. Target heart rate zones are determined by a percentage of an individual's maximum heart rate. The most accurate way of calculating these zones is by going for lactate threshold testing, which involves measuring blood lactate levels at various intensities. However, estimating your maximum heart rate using the formula 220 - age (in years) and then calculating percentages of this number is easy.

Percentage of Maximum Heart Rate	Intensity	Main Uses:
50-60%	Easy	Suitable for recovery or for enabling vast volumes of work with very low stress to the body.
60-70%	Steady	Training in this aerobic zone improves cardiovascular fitness and endurance by increasing the heart and lungs' capacity and the number and size of the mitochondria in muscle cells.
70-80%	Moderate - Hard	The level of intensity at which the body starts transitioning from aerobic to anaerobic metabolism. It improves the body's ability to use oxygen more efficiently.
80-90%	Hard - Very hard	This zone enhances specific performance attributes, including power, speed, and endurance, through brief yet intense intervals. At this intensity level, the body generates a substantial amount of lactic acid, which results in muscle fatigue.
90-100%	Maximum	Typically only sustainable for a short duration. The highest level of intensity there is. This will often be used for testing or racing.

Tracking your heart rate is essential to utilise these heart rate zones effectively during training. The most reliable method for doing so is by using a heart rate monitor. Heart rate monitors compatible with the Concept2 rowing machine include Polar and Garmin. For accurate results, use a chest strap-style heart rate monitor and ensure that it is wet enough to maintain a good connection.

My indoor rowing plans all have workout intensities specified. These can be performed solely based on your perceived rate of exertion and how hard you feel you're working, or if you think you'd like to incorporate a heart rate monitor into your training, you can assume the following heart rate zones for the intensities listed:

- Steady: 60-70%

- Moderate: 70-80%

- Hard: 80-90%

- Very hard: 85-95%

- Maximal: 90-100%

The 50-60% zone (Sometimes called UT2) is prevalent amongst rowers. However, I recommend that steady sessions be completed at 60-70%, which provides better results to most clients. 50-60% is best for elite rowers and professional athletes whose training regimens include up to 3 training sessions per day, six days per week. These individuals need to perform much of their training at lower intensities to maintain such high volumes of work and avoid burnout.

I recommend using 50-60% for sessions longer than 90 minutes, e.g. training for endurance events such as rowing marathons.

WHERE TO LOOK FOR INDOOR ROWING PROGRAMMING

Like any training, you must invest in excellent programming to take your performance to the next level. In its most basic form, this can be inexpensive and surprisingly accessible.

An excellent indoor rowing plan will incorporate progressive overload, which involves gradually increasing the demands of the exercise over time to elicit continuous performance improvements. However, a truly effective program goes beyond physical progression and includes psychological advancement. By strategically overloading the workouts, it is possible to develop an athlete's mental toughness, helping them push through mental barriers and change their perception of effort.

Another essential advantage of programming is that it helps ensure a balanced training approach across all energy systems. Depending on an individual's goals, specific energy systems may need to be emphasised over others. For instance, if an individual is training for an endurance event, their programming will likely prioritise aerobic training. Conversely, anaerobic and power training may be emphasised if preparing for a sprint race. Specificity is a critical aspect of training, and a coach can help design programs that target the correct energy systems to optimise performance.

Please visit my website for details of my indoor rowing programmes and coaching services: *cattrenthampersonaltraining.com.*

INPUTTING YOUR WORKOUTS INTO THE PERFORMANCE MONITOR

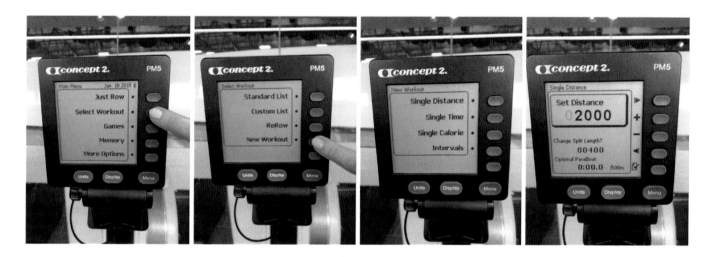

After selecting an indoor rowing training plan, it's crucial to familiarise yourself with inputting your workouts into the rowing machine. Programming your workouts can be done in one of two ways: on the performance monitor itself or the ErgData app.

If you program your workout on the performance monitor, you will have two options: 'Just Row' or 'Select Workout'. 'Just Row' resets all numbers to zero and starts counting time and distance immediately. This is a quick and easy option; it is suitable for warm-ups and cool-downs but not recommended for your main workout. Instead, it's better to choose 'Select Workout' to program your training more accurately.

Upon clicking the 'Select Workout' button, you will be presented with several options:

- Starting a new workout.
- Re-rowing a past workout.
- Choosing from a list of favourite workouts (including a standard list and a custom list for adding your favourites).

Typically, you will opt for a 'New Workout', where you can select from various options such as 'Single Distance', 'Single Time', 'Single Calories', or 'Intervals'.

For 'Single Distance', 'Single Time', or 'Single Calories', enter the work to be completed and make any adjustments to the default split length if necessary. Adjusting the default split length can help you interpret your results better in the summary screen at the end of your workout. There are exceptions, but the performance monitor typically divides your score into 20% blocks; this may only sometimes be useful.

E.g. If you were to do a single distance workout of 500m, your summary screen would show you your score with a breakdown at every 100m; this is very useful. However, for some workouts, e.g. a single time of 40-minutes with stroke rate changes every 10-minutes, it's more helpful to view your results in 10-minute splits to see if you achieved your desired stroke rates rather than the default 8-minute splits, which can make it tricky to interpret your results. For this reason, it's sometimes necessary to adjust the default split length to suit the workout better and improve the accuracy of your results.

When you select 'Intervals', you can choose from distance, time, calorie, or variable intervals. Distance, time, and calorie intervals are examples of constant intervals, whereby the work and rest times are the same for every repetition. Select the relevant category for your desired interval type and enter the work and rest times. For example, if you want to do 10 x 250m with 1.30 rests, you would choose distance intervals and input 250m for the work and 1.30 for the rest. The performance monitor will tell you which repetition you are on during your workout. Once you have completed all repetitions, press 'Menu' to end the workout and stop the monitor from counting up to an extra repetition.

For variable intervals, you must input the work and rest times for each interval individually. After inputting each interval, the monitor will prompt you to add another or select 'No More Intervals.' Accuracy is crucial when inputting variable intervals into the monitor. To avoid mistakes and ensure precision, I recommended using the ErgData app for programming your workout; it is easier and enables you to detect and correct errors more effortlessly.

If you choose to use the ErgData app, connect your phone to the performance monitor and program the workout from your phone. Enter the distance or time, desired split length, and rest time. In most instances, you can ignore the options for 'show pacer', 'target stroke rate', and 'target HR zone'.

THE ERGDATA APP

ErgData is a great free app you can download for your phone. It connects to the performance monitor via Bluetooth. It makes programming and recording your workouts much easier! It also records additional stroke-by-stroke data and synchronises automatically to a Concept2 logbook (more on these later). The ErgData app displays additional information to the performance monitor. Two valuable examples of this are 'Drive Length' and 'Stroke Count'.

Drive length measures the distance the chain moves during the drive phase of each stroke. It is a good tool for ensuring consistent technique. We will look at this in more detail later.

Stroke count can be a valuable metric for specific stroke rate sessions, which we will discuss later. For instance, if you are performing a 30-minute workout with a stroke rate of 20 strokes per minute, aiming for a stroke count which is a multiple of 20 by the end of each minute can help you stay on track.

The best way to display ErgData so you can see it whilst rowing is to invest in a smartphone cradle to place on top of the performance monitor. These can be purchased from the Concept2 online shop.

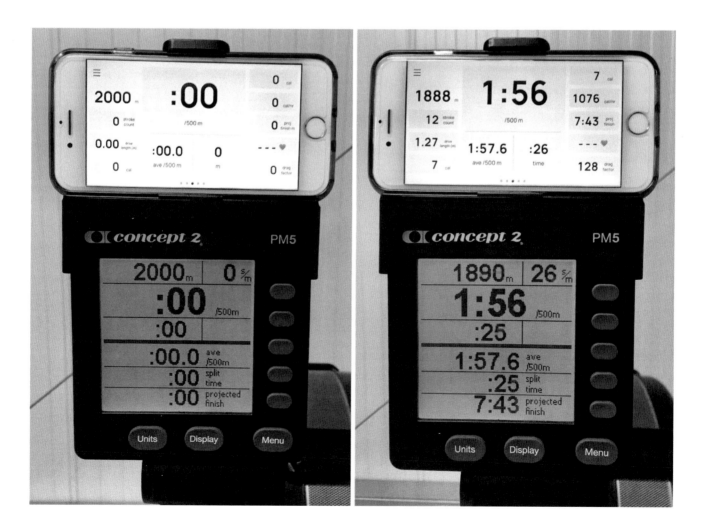

CONNECTING ERGDATA

ErgData is designed to be used with a free Concept2 online logbook. When you set up your ErgData account, follow the on-screen instructions to 'Connect to Logbook'; this will connect your ErgData app to your Logbook account.

To pair your ErgData app with the PM5 monitor, ensure Bluetooth is turned on on your device and within range of the PM5 (which should also be turned on).

Your ErgData app should be on the 'Workout' page. Select the top option: 'Connect to a Performance Monitor (PM5)'. From here, it will show the ID numbers of PM5s in range and the relevant icon if they are a RowErg, SkiErg or BikeErg. If only a single option shows, click 'Tap to Connect'. If you are in a gym or rowing club where it is showing options for lots of machines, you can press the 'Connect' button on the PM5; this will show you the PM5 ID, and you can select the matching one from your list on ErgData. Once your device is paired with the PM5 monitor, you can input your workout and should be able to see your workout data on the ErgData app in real-time as you row.

To avoid issues for the following user in a commercial setting and prevent false workouts from appearing in your logbook, disconnect from ErgData after your workout. Disconnecting will also help conserve the battery life of the performance monitor and ensure it turns off after periods of inactivity. You can do this on the app or by pressing the monitor's menu button four times in a row.

DRIVE LENGTH

Drive length measures the distance the chain moves during the drive phase of each stroke. Your drive length will depend upon your height, limb length, flexibility and the efficiency of your technique. It will be different for each athlete. It can be helpful to know roughly where you'd expect yours to be, and then you can use it to help you gauge consistency in your technique, especially as fatigue begins to set in! If your drive length suddenly reduces, it could indicate that you are not sitting tall or rocking forwards enough in the recovery phase and are missing out on length at the catch.

Analysing the numbers from multiple sessions when feeling relatively fresh will allow you to recognise a consistent number for your optimal drive length.

If you look at the pictures below, you will see that the best way to optimise length at the front end (catch) is to ensure you're sitting tall, not slumped, and in a rocked forward position; this is usually where most length is lost. The best way to optimise length at the Back end (finish) is to ensure you are sat tall with a slight lean back. Ensuring the handle is pulled to the lower chest rather than the waist is not only good practice and more efficient, but it's good for a few additional drive length centimetres too!

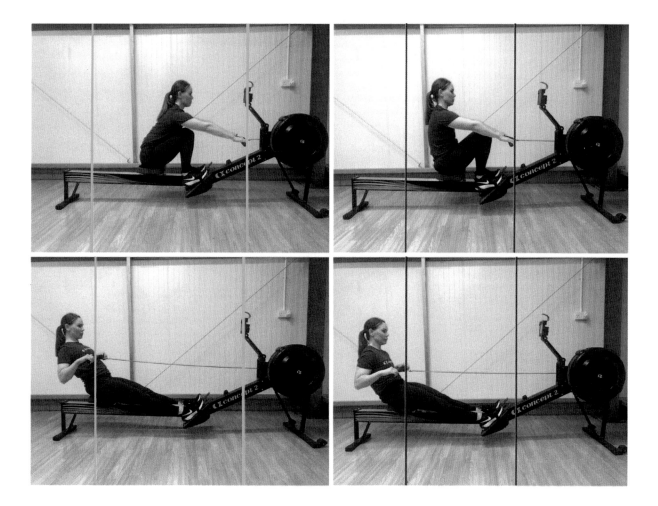

UNDERSTANDING THE PM5 DISPLAY

DISPLAY

You can change the display layout by pressing the display button in the centre at the bottom of the performance monitor. The all-data screen shows the most data and is the best setting for most workouts. Other options include the force curve screen, a pace boat screen, a bar chart screen and a large print screen.

The All-Data Screen

The all-data screen shows the most data so is the best setting for most workouts.

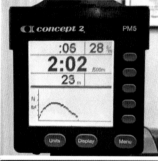

Force Curve Screen

The force curve screen provides a graphic representation of how force is applied throughout the stroke. The objective is to produce a bell-shaped curve with a high peak and plenty of surface area beneath it. A smooth curve generally indicates efficient force transmission throughout the stroke sequence, while a large surface area beneath the curve signifies the application of significant force.

Whilst this can be useful, I would recommend it for warm-ups rather than workouts, where the all-data screen is preferable to enable you to view more of the available data.

Examining the three examples, we can observe the following:

Top photo: A smooth, bell-shaped curve representing efficient rowing.

Middle photo: Peaks in the force curve typically indicate inefficient sequencing and suboptimal power transfer.

Bottom photo: A force curve resembling this implies that the legs contribute minimal power while the arms and shoulders perform most of the work.

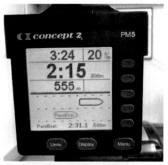

Pace Boat Screen

The pace boat screen serves two purposes: setting a target pace for a new workout and displaying the speed of your previous attempt if you are repeating a workout. Whilst this can be useful, be aware that it may only be somewhat helpful, as your target splits may vary throughout the workout. A detailed pacing strategy from your rowing coach will provide better accuracy and yield better overall results.

Bar chart screen

The bar chart screen typically displays a visual representation of your power output in watts during your workout. A higher bar corresponds to a higher power output. If you have connected a heart rate monitor, the bar chart will display your heart rate instead, with a higher bar indicating a higher heart rate.

Large print screen

The large print screen can be helpful to anyone needing help seeing the smaller numbers. The available data is reduced, but the central values can all be viewed.

UNITS

The PM5 provides various unit options, such as calories, watts, meters, and pace, which you can change by pressing the 'units' button and cycling through the options.

For a clear comparison of workouts with different lengths, use the time per 500 meters (0.00/500m) metric. Lower numbers indicate faster rowing and quicker distance coverage. Set your units to meters or pace to view this metric.

For example, if you completed a 5000m row with an average pace of 2.16.0/500m, and a week later, you completed a 6000m row with an average pace of 2.14.5/500m, you can see that you are getting faster and stronger because the time it takes you to cover each 500m is decreasing, even though the distance is longer.

Pace (Time per 500m) is also essential for calculating pacing strategies.

| Meters | Pace | Watts | Calories |

THE PM5 SCREEN

If using 'Just Row,' this box will display time and count up. If your workout is programmed in, the value here will count down.
In interval workouts, the rest time will be displayed here, followed by the letter r; this will count down to your next interval.

The number of strokes per minute (s/m)

If you maintained the same pace, this would be the time it would take you to row 500m.
During the rest period in interval workouts, it will show you the number of intervals completed so far.

CI concept 2.

Time / Distance / Calories / Rest	Stroke Rate
Current Split Time (Time/500m)	
Time / Distance / Calories	Heart Rate
Overall Split Time (Time/500m)	
Split Meters / Intervals	
Predicted Finish Score	

This box is usually empty; this is where your heart rate will display if you wear a monitor.

For me, this is the most critical value of all; **this is the average time taken to row 500m throughout your workout.** The lower the number, the faster your score.

The number interval you are on, or your split meters. (Eg. If you were to do a 40-minute row with a split length of 10 minutes, this would show the distance achieved in the current 10-minute window.)

Units   Display

This will display meters and count upwards for timed workouts, timed intervals, or a 'Just Row' piece. For distance pieces/distance intervals or calorie workouts, it will display time, which will also count upward.

This is calculated based on your average split time so far and your current split time. For a single time or distance, it will predict the score for the entire completion. For intervals, it will be for each repetition.
(During the rest, it will show the total meters achieved, including rollover meters.)
For 'Just Row', it will predict the number of meters you can achieve in 30 minutes. If you continue to row beyond this, it will predict for 60 minutes and so on.

RECORDING YOUR RESULTS

At the end of your workout, press 'Menu' to take you back to the main menu. (If doing an interval session, do this before it rolls over into another repetition.)

To view your completed workout, select 'Memory' (on older machines, you need to go to 'More Options' and then 'Memory'), and then choose 'List by Date'. The most recent workout will appear at the top of the list and should already be selected. However, if you want to view an older workout, use the arrow buttons to navigate up or down the list. Once you locate the desired workout, press the button next to the magnifying glass icon to display the summary screen. The summary screen may extend over multiple pages if your workout includes numerous intervals or short split lengths. You can scroll through them using the arrow buttons, split by split or page by page.

Make it a habit to photograph your summary screen after each workout. This way, you can easily refer back to your scores when needed. If you want to review a summary screen from a non-recent, past workout on the performance monitor, you can use the 'List by Type' function and enter details of the workout. However, this may not be ideal in a commercial gym or rowing club setting where multiple machines are available due to the challenges of identifying the correct machine and workout. Moreover, there's a possibility of mistaking someone else's training for yours. Taking photos as part of your post-row routine is always the best option!

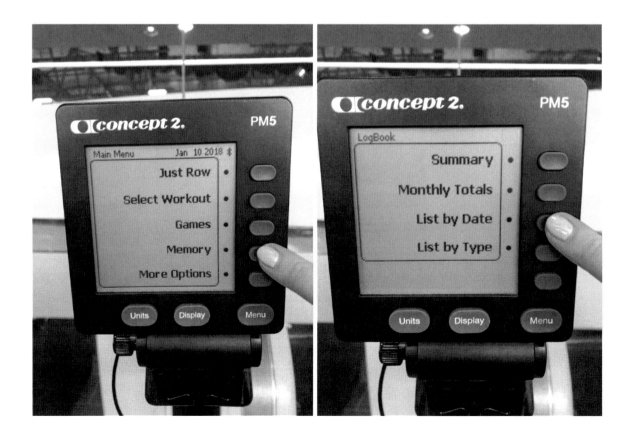

MAKING SENSE OF YOUR RESULTS

SUMMARY AND SPLITS

Your summary screen will show you a summary of your workout and individual splits. The numbers in the top row between the two horizontal lines show the summary, and the rows below show the splits.

The summary will show the total duration of your row, the total distance covered, your average split time (time/500m), your average strokes per minute (and your average heart rate if you had a heart rate monitor connected). Pressing the Units button at the bottom of the screen will allow you to view total calories, calories per hour or watts instead of pace (time/500m), should you want to. The summary shows you your totals and averages for the entire piece.

The splits are where we can see detail from the workout and any pace changes which occurred throughout. Unless you programmed your workout with a specific split length, the monitor usually shows your workout in 20% sections (with a few exceptions). If you have done an interval workout, each split will be one interval. Increases or decreases in pace and strokes per minute will give your coach a good idea of how your row is going in different sections and determine where improvements can be made.

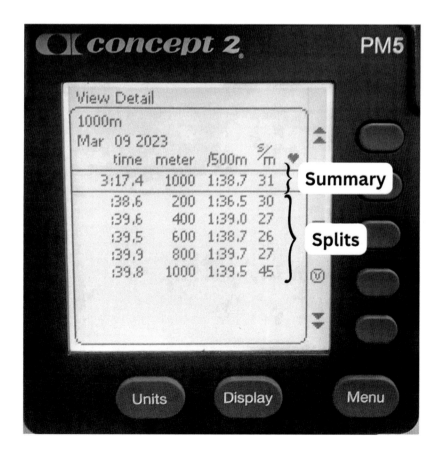

POSITIVE, NEGATIVE AND EVEN SPLITS

Positive Splits

To have positive splits in a workout means the pace gets slower as you get further through the workout.

Like in the example shown, it might be that each interval gets gradually slower, or if it's one continuous piece, it might be that the pace gets slower throughout the workout.

Negative Splits

Negative splits are the opposite. With negative splits, the pace would get faster as the workout progresses.

Again, it could be an interval session, with each interval being faster than the previous one. Or it could be a continuous piece whereby each section is faster than the previous.

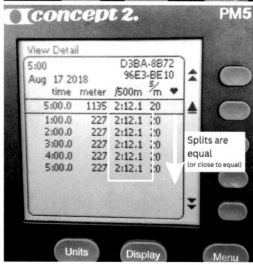

Even Splits

Even splits stay constant throughout, with no intentional pace increases or decreases.

You can have fun with these by aiming for OCD summary screens, as pictured here!

For a true OCD screen, the total meters must equal the sum of all the split meters with no rounding errors! They are renowned for being tricky to achieve!

VERIFICATION CODES

A Concept2 verification code is a 16-digit number used to verify workouts sent as record submissions. It can also be nice to verify the workouts you are adding to the rankings on your Concept2 logbook, as they give additional credibility. It is essential to check that the date on your monitor is set correctly before completing your row, as this will form part of the data in the verification code. (To access the 'Date and Time' settings, go to the main menu, select 'More Options,' 'Utilities,' and then 'Date and Time.')

If you use the ErgData app, all workouts will automatically have a verification code. To manually obtain a verification code, press the fourth button, which is indicated by a little 'v' symbol on newer machines. There won't be any symbol on older devices, and you must press the button twice. The verification code will appear at the top right of the screen.

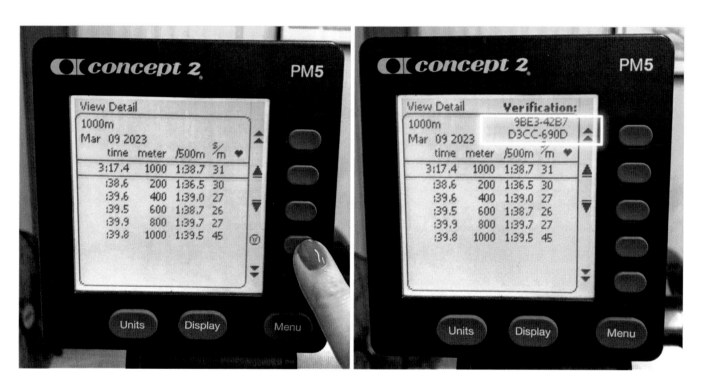

ROLLOVER METERS

Rollover meters refer to any meters achieved during a workout which do not contribute towards your score. We see a lot of rollover meters when performing interval sessions; this is because the flywheel continues to spin for a few seconds after we stop exerting force through the handle, and the machine continues to clock meters.

Rollover meters are displayed at the bottom of your summary screen, beneath your final split from the workout. You will see the letter r, followed by the number of meters.

These can be useful for your coach when looking through your interval session. If your session was high-speed sprints and you had very few rollover meters, it is usually a sign that you were stopping or slowing down before the repetition was complete, which can be costly to your result. Conversely, high rollover meters would be a sign that you were doing more work than you needed to be and were rowing way into the rest time, therefore reducing your recovery time unnecessarily, which could also be costly when aiming for optimised performance.

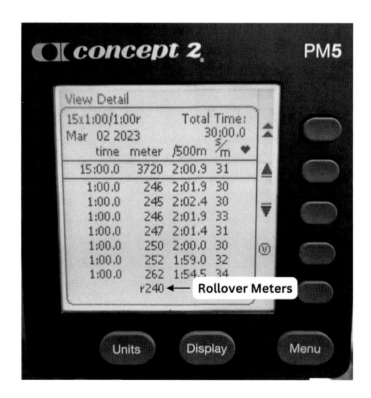

CONCEPT 2 ONLINE LOGBOOK, RANKINGS AND MILLION-METER CLUBS

Register for a complimentary online logbook on the Concept2 website to keep track of your workouts and cumulative meters. The ErgData app streamlines this process by automatically syncing all workout details when you connect it to the performance monitor before commencing your training.

You can view your lifetime personal bests in the 'history' section of the online logbook, making them very accessible. You can also compare your performances to others worldwide by ranking your scores for certain distances and timed workouts. It is easy to filter by age, gender, and weight class to see how you stack up against others. This feature can be a great source of motivation to help you improve your scores and reach your goals.

The online logbook also automatically tracks your total cumulative meters, which can be found in the 'Challenges' section under 'RowErg Million Meter Club'. This feature can vastly incentivise reaching a million meters or more. You can download a certificate from the Concept2 website for every million meters reached. In addition, Concept2 rewards participants with free enamelled pins and clothing at some of the more significant milestones (1 million, 5 million, 10 million etc.) There is no time limit to achieve these milestones; you can work towards them at your own pace. Remember to log all your meters, including warm-ups and cool-downs, to help you reach these milestones faster!

STROKE RATE

Stroke rate is the number of strokes completed per minute. In some rowing workouts, keeping to a particular stroke rate or a series of specified stroke rates may be necessary.

The stroke rate is displayed in the screen's top right or bottom left corner, depending on how you set the display. It is the two-digit number followed by 's/m' for strokes per minute.

Improving your control over stroke rates is critical for mastering pacing during rowing. A common mistake among beginner rowers is assuming that simply pushing harder will lead to better scores. In reality, pushing harder beyond a certain point can result in a breakdown of technical efficiency rather than an increase in speed. Increasing power per stroke and manipulating stroke rates is necessary for control and optimal performance.

Pace typically increases as the stroke rate increases and decreases as the stroke rate reduces (assuming good technique and effort are applied). Stroke rates should always be the primary metric for adjusting your pace. However, there is a limit to how many strokes per minute can be comfortably performed, especially during longer sessions. Slower stroke rates are more sustainable during longer-duration workouts and offer an excellent opportunity to focus on enhancing technique and increasing your power per stroke.

Increasing power per stroke is crucial for achieving better scores in indoor rowing, as it means producing more watts and covering more distance with each stroke. While this takes time, it is worth the effort! Increasing either your power per stroke or stroke rate will result in a quicker pace; increasing both together will result in something very rapid!

Power per stroke x Number of strokes = Pace

When attempting to row at a desired stroke rate for the first time, it can be challenging to maintain a consistent pace or even reach the target number at all. Similarly, generating power may be difficult when rowing more slowly than you're used to. However, with practice, you will improve surprisingly quickly. It is worth persevering on this, as mastery will open the door to outstanding scores.

Things to think about when learning how to control your stroke rate:

- Adjust your stroke rate by adjusting the duration of the recovery phase. Your drive and recovery phases do not need to be the same duration. Your drive phase should be explosive and quick, regardless of your stroke rate. The recovery phase is where you can make the necessary adjustments. E.g. If you were to row at 20 strokes per minute (s/m), this equates to one complete stroke every 3 seconds. 1 second of this might be the drive phase, and 2 seconds might be the recovery phase. Whereas a stroke rate of 24s/m would equate to 1 complete stroke every 2.5 seconds, so in this instance, the drive phase would be 1 second, and the recovery would be 1.5 seconds. The drive phase should remain relatively constant and only increase for sprint pieces at high stroke rates where the range of motion reduces to allow for a faster stroke rate.

- Tools like ErgData can help, as you can input target strokes per minute, and there is also a stroke counter. If you were doing a 30-minute workout at 20 strokes per minute, you would expect your total strokes to be a multiple of 20 at each minute (or a multiple of 10 at each 30-second window) to be on track.

- Rowing metronomes can also be an option.

- If you are doing a workout with varying stroke rates, it can be helpful to calculate the times/distances at which the change in stroke rates will occur before beginning your row. Writing these down and placing them somewhere you can see them can be helpful. A small whiteboard leaning against a wall in front of your rower or a small piece of paper taped to the bottom of your monitor can work well.

Unless you are using the stroke count feature on ErgData and watching it fairly avidly, you won't be able to see how successful your stroke rate attempts were until you get to the end of your workout and look at your summary screen. Strokes per minute are displayed in the right-hand column.

Here is a 10-minute stroke rate pyramid with 2-minute splits aiming for r18/r20/r22/r20/r18.

The first 2 minutes are done at r18 (18 strokes per minute), the next 2 minutes at r20 and so on.

You can see that all stroke rates have been achieved by looking in the far right column on the summary screen, which shows 18,20,22,20,18.

Notice how at each rate increase, the pace also increases, and at each rate decrease, the pace decreases.

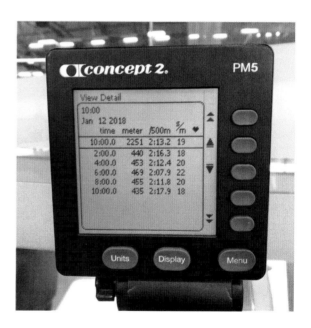

UNDERSTANDING PACING TARGETS

Your pacing target for a workout will likely relate to your overall average pace, your average pace per 500m for the entire workout.

Your target pace might be determined by one of your previous scores; this may be written in several ways:

- **2k+1.** If you see your target pace written as 2k+1, you should aim to maintain a pace one second slower than the average pace you held for your most recent 2000m best. E.g. If your most recent time for 2000m were 8 minutes exactly, your average pace per 500m would have been 2.00.0. Therefore, your 2k+1 pace would be 2.01.0/500m.

- **2k-1.** Your 2k-1 time in this scenario would be 1.59.0/500m

- **2k+20.** And your 2k+20 score would be 2.20.0/500m

Sometimes, the target pace may be expressed differently and be based on a recent workout if you still need to establish scores for important benchmark pieces. E.g.

- **Target: within 1 second of last week's score.** If your score for the previous week was 2.13.1/500m, then your goal for the new workout should be 2.14.1/500m or better.

- **Target: within 0.5 of a second of last week's score.** If your score for the previous week was 1.48.2/500m, then your goal for the new workout should be 1.48.7/500m or better.

These workouts typically increase in volume each week; the aim is to maintain a consistent pace despite the added workload.

Sometimes you will see the targets written like this:

- **Target: 2 seconds faster than last week's score.** If your score from last week were 2.34.0/500m, your target this week would be 2.32.0/500m.

PREDICTED FINISH SCORE

Predicted finish scores can be instrumental in helping you to achieve your target if used appropriately. It shows your estimated finish score based on the work you have completed so far (overall average) and the pace you are currently at (current average).

Your predicted finish score will likely fluctuate drastically in the early stages of your workout. When you are fresh, it will show something faster than what you are truly capable of. A 500m test piece is an excellent example of this. These are generally performed with positive splits for maximal performance. Getting too hung up on the predicted finish score too early can lure you into a false sense of expectation when you should be paying more attention to your pacing and strategy. Your predicted finish score is of more use in the final 150m of a 500m test when you're trying to ensure that the drop-off in pace is minimal and the score you want is still within reach. In this instance, the predicted finish score can be a good incentive and motivator.

For many workouts, instead of solely chasing a predicted finish score, I recommend using the Concept2 pace calculator to help work out a suitable pace if you have a specific time goal for your workout.

CONCEPT2 PACE CALCULATOR

The Concept2 pace calculator is a great free tool, which can be found on the Concept2 website. Check that the calculator is set to 'Indoor Rower' mode at the top before use (unless you intend to use it for the BikeErg).

To calculate either time, distance, or pace, you must know the other two variables.

E.g. To determine the pace required to complete a 2000m row in 6.30, input the distance (2000m) and time (6:30) into the calculator; this will enable you to calculate the required pace, expressed as a 500m split (1:37.5/500m).

You can also use this calculator for other purposes. For instance, if you have a target pace for a distance workout, you can calculate the duration of the session so you know how much time you need to set aside to complete it.

Similarly, try the Concept2 pace chart on the Concept2 website to help predict your total time/distance at a given pace.

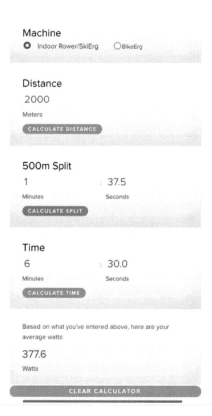

RECOVERY BETWEEN SESSIONS

Given the physical demands of rowing, it is essential to prioritise rest and recovery. While it can be tempting to keep pushing through, recovery is vital for optimising performance.

Recovery time is beneficial in many ways:

- It allows your body to adapt to training stress by repairing damaged tissues and building new ones, thereby increasing strength and endurance, vital to rowing performance.

- Rest allows your nervous system a chance to recover, which can help prevent over-training and burnout.

- Taking a break from training is also profoundly beneficial from a psychological standpoint. It can reduce stress, improve mood and increase motivation. It provides an opportunity for mental preparation, reflection on performance and goal setting.

Ignoring the need for sufficient recovery, or failing to prioritise it, can put you at risk of increased injury, excessive fatigue and a decline in performance. Even if you do other sports or training alongside rowing, you should aim for a minimum of 1-2 rest days per week. It is ideal to spread multiple rest days throughout the week rather than taking them all in one go. I recommend taking rest days directly before high-intensity workout days, particularly if you have a race or a test piece scheduled, to ensure you feel as fresh as possible. To further manage fatigue, distribute your high-intensity workouts evenly throughout the week and intersperse them with steadier sessions.

OTHER TRAINING ALONGSIDE INDOOR ROWING

Incorporating other training alongside indoor rowing can be very beneficial, but doing so in a way that complements rowing performance and recovery is essential. One type of training that pairs well with indoor rowing is weight training, as it helps to build muscle strength, thereby helping with increasing power per stroke.

Squats, deadlifts, leg presses, seated rows, seal rows and pull-ups can be particularly effective. Abdominal exercises, such as planks and rollouts, offer significant benefits by enhancing core strength, which is crucial for maintaining proper posture and positioning during rowing. A strong core will help you to sit tall without slumping, as well as assist you in transmitting your power effectively throughout the sequence of the stroke.

When incorporating other types of training alongside indoor rowing, it is essential to use suitable progressions and keep work volume appropriate to avoid excessive muscle soreness, which can negatively impact indoor rowing workouts. Exercise bikes or SkiErgs can be good options for other cardiovascular training that won't cause excessive muscle soreness. Running or circuit training with lots of jumping and plyometric movements is not recommended, as they can cause a lot of muscle soreness.

I recommend combining weight training (or other activities) with indoor rowing 1-2 times per week, enabling you to reap the benefits while reducing the risk of injury or over-training.

NUTRITION, HYDRATION AND SLEEP

Focusing on nutrition, hydration, and sleep is essential to get the most out of your indoor rowing workouts. Optimising nutrition and hydration can enhance your performance and promote faster recovery.

NUTRITION

Calories: Your daily calorie needs will depend on gender, age, weight, height and activity level. As a general guideline, adult women engaged in regular indoor rowing may need between 1800-2500 calories per day, while adult men may need anywhere from 2500-3500 per day. Individual needs vary widely. To better understand your personalised needs, consider working with a nutrition coach or using free online tools like a BMR calculator and the Harris-Benedict Formula to help estimate your calorie needs based on the criteria mentioned above.

If you are trying to lose weight while following an indoor rowing program, ensure your calorie deficit is sensible and not too extreme. Remember that you need to eat enough to support your activity levels, and eliminating food groups can do more harm than good. It is perfectly possible to lose weight on a balanced diet, which will nourish your body and fuel your performance. Anything overly restrictive will not only feel miserable, but it will likely reduce athletic performance.

Carbohydrates: Carbohydrates are an essential fuel source for high-intensity exercise like indoor rowing. Aim to consume between 3-5 grams of carbohydrates per kilogram of body weight per day. For example, a 70kg rower would need between 210-350 grams of carbohydrates daily. Good sources of carbohydrates include rice, oats, potatoes, fruits, vegetables, and legumes.

Protein: Protein is essential for muscle repair, growth and recovery. It will help your muscles to recover properly between workouts. Aim to consume between 1.4-2.2 grams of protein per kilogram of body weight daily. For example, a 70kg rower would need 98-154 grams of protein daily. Good protein sources include lean meats, poultry, fish, eggs, dairy, and protein shakes. Protein can also be found in smaller quantities in plant-based sources like beans, lentils, and tofu.

For additional help with nutrition, visit cattrenthampersonaltraining. com*.*

HYDRATION

Proper hydration is essential for achieving optimal indoor rowing performance. Dehydration can lead to decreased performance, fatigue, cramps, and even injury during workouts; it is crucial to maintain good hydration levels throughout the day, not just during exercise.

I recommend drinking water regularly and adding electrolyte tablets to your water during long, sweaty indoor rowing sessions, particularly during warmer weather. Popular options include 'High5 Zero' tablets containing potassium and sodium to help maintain hydration levels. Adding one electrolyte tablet to 500ml of water is a good starting point, but individuals should adjust this based on their sweat rate and body weight. (Before adding any electrolytes, it is vital to check that these will not interfere with any medications or pre-existing health conditions).

In addition to drinking water and electrolyte solutions, other ways to maintain good hydration levels include consuming lots of water-rich foods like fruits and vegetables and using hydration trackers.

Deciding when to drink during a row is a personal choice that depends on several factors, such as your goals, abilities, and session length. You might not need to pause for a drink if you're doing a row of 10k or less or one that lasts 40 minutes or less. For instance, during a 10k test, stopping for a drink could hurt your score, so it's crucial to ensure you are correctly hydrated beforehand and replenish fluids as soon as the workout is finished.

For longer rows, consider taking a quick sip every 4k or so. Beginners may prefer to drink more frequently, perhaps every 3k, while faster male rowers, who can cover more distance more quickly, may choose to drink less often, maybe every 5k. If you're doing an interval session, it's usually best to take small sips between intervals rather than large gulps, which can cause nausea when rests are short. As with long rows, ensure you are hydrated before and after the workout. Ultimately, the key is finding the best for you based on your needs and preferences. Experiment with different drinking strategies to find what works best for your body and goals.

To monitor hydration levels, individuals can check their urine colour or weight before and after exercise. A pale yellow or clear urine colour indicates good hydration, while darker yellow or amber urine may indicate dehydration. Checking body weight before and after exercise can also estimate fluid loss and help individuals determine how much water and electrolytes they need to replenish. However, these methods are only somewhat accurate. Additional methods for monitoring hydration levels include measuring heart rate variability or tracking thirst levels.

SLEEP

Getting sufficient and quality sleep is crucial for optimising indoor rowing performance. When we sleep, our bodies repair and grow muscle tissue, essential for maintaining physical fitness. Inadequate sleep can elevate the risk of injury and hormonal imbalances, hindering metabolism and energy levels and reducing performance.

It is recommended that adults aim for 7-9 hours of sleep each night to support optimal health and performance. You can improve your sleep quality in several ways:

- Try to establish a consistent sleep routine whereby you go to bed and wake up at the same time every day, even on weekends; this can help regulate your body's internal clock and improve sleep quality.
- Try to limit caffeine and alcohol intake, especially before bedtime, as they can disrupt your sleep.
- Aim to reduce your screen time in the hour before bed.
- Create a comfortable sleeping environment. Make sure your bedroom is quiet, calm, and dark. Invest in a comfortable, supportive mattress and pillows.
- Consider practising relaxation techniques such as meditation or deep breathing before bedtime to help calm your mind and promote better sleep.

COMPETITIONS

Competitive indoor rowing can be a great way to challenge yourself and push your limits. If you want to participate in races, the Concept2 and British Rowing websites are excellent resources for finding information on competitions in your area.

Typically, indoor rowing races are held during winter, the off-season for on-water rowers. The two main race distances are the 2000m and 500m events. During these races, you will compete against others in your gender, age, and weight class. Some larger competitions also host a range of adaptive classes.

WEIGHT CLASSES

Regarding weight classes, there are usually only two: lightweight and heavyweight. The lightweight class is for men weighing 75.0kg or less and women weighing 61.5kg or less. Everyone else will enter the heavyweight category.

If you are within 1-2kg of the lightweight limit, it may be worth temporarily losing a little weight to compete in this category, where your scores may be more competitive. However, never compromise your health to pursue a lower weight class. Do this over several weeks so that only a slight calorie deficit is needed. Reducing weight via dehydration is not advised, as there is not enough time between weigh-in and racing to rehydrate, which may negatively affect performance.

Notably, the fastest scores usually come from the heavyweight categories because mass moves mass. This class often includes taller competitors with longer limbs, who can travel further with each stroke.

WHAT TO EXPECT AT YOUR FIRST RACE

Preparing for your first indoor rowing race can be exciting and nerve-wracking, but being prepared can help you feel confident on race day. Here are some things you can expect at your first race:

First, arrive with plenty of time for registration and a good warm-up. You should have already been assigned a rowing machine, so double-check which one it is. At some larger races, you may be allocated a warm-up time, the only time you can access a rowing machine ahead of your actual race, so take advantage of it. At other races, there may be a bank of warm-up machines that you can access as needed. Give yourself a few minutes between warming up and racing to allow your heart rate and breathing chance to settle.

You must weigh in if you're competing in the lightweight category. Depending on the competition, you may need to have a photo ID with you when you do this. Weigh-in is usually between 1 and 2 hours before the start of your race. Doing this as soon as possible is a good idea, especially if you are close to the weight limit; this will give you additional time to visit the toilet or run around the block in multiple layers of clothes to try to make weight if you need to!

During the race, you will notice that the PM5 display differs from what you're accustomed to seeing. That is because all the machines will be linked to a race system which enables you to track your progress relative to your competitors. The top half of the PM5 will show your regular workout data; the bottom half will display your current position in the race, plus details of the leader and the rowers immediately ahead and behind you, including the distance (in meters) by which they are leading or trailing. If you're leading the race, you'll see the second-place rower and the distance they are behind you. This information is typically projected onto a large screen for spectators to follow the event.

After arriving at your race machine, you'll have a few minutes to prepare the rowing machine to your usual specifications before starting the race. Remember to do this if you're used to using a privately-owned rowing machine that is always set up and ready for you! Start by adjusting the foot stretchers to your preferred height and adjusting the drag factor. Note that you won't be able to set the drag factor in the usual way or connect to ErgData during the race since the PM5 will be connected to the race system. However, you can manually log your score onto your Concept2 logbook if you take a reference photo of your finish screen at the end of the race. The drag factor will be displayed on the PM5 screen, and you can view it by rowing a few strokes without pressing any buttons. Make sure to change it to your preferred setting.

At the beginning of the race, the PM5 display will show 'Sit Ready', followed by 'Attention', and then 'Row'. As soon as you see the 'Row' command, start rowing promptly. It is essential to avoid rowing before the 'Row' command, as doing so will result in a false start and require the procedure to be repeated.

When racing, your overall pace will be based on your reaction time at the start as well as your rowing speed, so don't be alarmed if you notice a slower overall average on the first few strokes than you are used to seeing in practice. Stick to your pacing plan and trust that your average speed will improve after a few strokes.

My top advice for anyone participating in an indoor rowing race is to stay committed to your pacing plan and avoid getting distracted by the actions of other competitors. Many people make the mistake of starting too aggressively (fly and die) and fading rapidly in the latter half of the race. By adhering to a well-planned pacing strategy, you could catch up and surpass other competitors in the final stretch.

Racing is an excellent opportunity to challenge yourself and gauge how you measure up against other indoor rowing enthusiasts in the community. If you're the type of person who enjoys a challenge, I would highly recommend it!

BASIC MAINTENANCE ADVICE

Owning a personal rowing machine comes with the responsibility of regular maintenance to guarantee its peak performance. Essential tasks include cleaning the monorail and seat rollers, lubricating the chain, removing debris from the flywheel, and updating the firmware. For an in-depth guide on maintaining your Concept2 RowErg, consult the Concept2 website, which provides extensive instructions and resources. The following are some fundamental maintenance steps you should perform:

WIPING DOWN THE MONORAIL AND SEAT ROLLERS

A smooth surface for the rowing seat to move on is crucial to ensure the smoothest possible glide. By wiping down the monorail, you can quickly and easily improve your rowing experience.

Over time, a black residue can accumulate on the monorail due to lubricant from the seat rollers, dirt, and sweat. Regularly cleaning off this residue is essential to maintain a smooth and aerodynamic surface. You can use either glass cleaner or soapy water to clean the monorail. Plain water and a paper towel will suffice if you use a gym rowing machine and the monorail needs cleaning.

When cleaning the monorail, be sure to clean the entire length and the seat rollers. To clean the seat rollers, hold a cloth against them while gently moving the seat back and forth. Be careful not to trap your fingers in the rollers! Cleaning the seat rollers is vital because they can accumulate black residue or become clogged with hair or grit. If the rollers aren't clean, rowing can become bumpy, and this sensation can hinder your performance. Cleaning the monorail and the seat rollers regularly ensures smoother, more effective workouts.

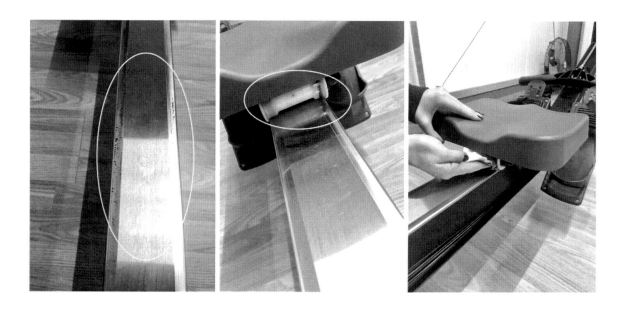

LUBRICATING THE CHAIN

Regularly oiling the chain is essential for maintaining the performance of your rowing machine. If you are a gym owner, lubrication should be done weekly, and for people with private machines, it should be done roughly once every 50 hours of use.

Apply approximately a teaspoon of 3 in 1 oil to an old rag or a paper towel. Next, pull the chain out entirely and apply the oil to the entire chain length as it slowly feeds back into the machine. This process may need repeating for machines that have not been oiled in a long time. Finally, wipe off excess oil to prevent it from attracting dirt and dust.

Regular lubrication can help keep the chain running smoothly and prevent it from wearing out prematurely. By making this routine part of your maintenance, you can ensure that your rowing machine is always in optimal condition for a great workout.

To prolong the life of your rowing machine's shock cords, try placing the handle against the chain guide whenever you are not actively rowing. Consider using the handle hook only during rest periods in intervals or other brief pauses during your workout.

KEEPING THE FLYWHEEL CLEAN

Keeping the flywheel clean is essential to prevent dust build-up in your rowing machine, which can reduce efficiency over time and require higher damper settings to achieve the same drag factor.

Removing the fan casing and vacuuming the flywheel after every 250 hours of use is recommended; this will help ensure that dust and debris don't accumulate inside the machine, causing it to run less efficiently.

Using a Phillips head screwdriver, loosen the four screws shown on the fan casing. Be sure to keep the small nuts that accompany them in a safe place.

The screw for the mesh perf can usually be found tucked behind the bottom right fastening. Loosen the screw holding the mesh outlet perf together, but don't fully undo it; this will allow the perf to rotate upwards so that you can access it more efficiently and allow for it to spring apart.

Assuming you are facing the fan, the mesh perf should be threaded out in an anti-clockwise direction. You will need to guide both ends of the perf.

Once this is out, this should be vacuumed/cleaned gently with a slightly damp cloth.

Remove the four outer screws and carefully lift off the front of the casing.
Use a vacuum cleaner or cloth to clean out the flywheel.

To replace the fan casing:

- Reverse the process.
- Put the case back in position and loosely attach the four screws around the edge.
- Thread the mesh perf back in a clockwise motion (the entry point is the middle right) and reattach the screw, tightening it loosely, then gently rotate the perf so that the join is hidden beneath the casing on the bottom right, then tighten the screw securely.
- Carefully secure the four outer screws, being careful not to over-tighten.

To test the effectiveness of the cleaning, perform four or five hard effort strokes with the damper set to 10 (the maximum); this will give you the maximum possible drag factor your machine is capable of.

Compare this value before and after cleaning the flywheel to see the difference.

UPDATING THE FIRMWARE

Updating the firmware on a Concept2 rowing machine is essential for ensuring the machine operates correctly and takes advantage of the latest features. Failing to update your firmware may lead to issues with the display, connectivity problems or workouts failing to save to the memory.

You can check on the Concept2 website if the firmware on your PM5 needs updating, or if you use ErgData, it will automatically alert you when a firmware update is available. Concept2 also have a mailing list on their website that you can join specifically for announcing firmware updates.

You can update the firmware on your Concept2 rowing machine directly through the ErgData app, or you can download and install the Concept2 Utility software on your computer. Connect your device using a USB cable or flash drive and follow the instructions in the software to install the latest firmware. Full instructions on updating the firmware can be found on the Concept2 website.

CHANGING THE BATTERIES IN THE PERFORMANCE MONITOR

To replace the batteries in the performance monitor, unscrew the thumb screw on the back and insert two new D-cell batteries. If you prefer, you can also use rechargeable D-cell batteries.

You can check the battery level by choosing 'More Options' from the main menu and then selecting 'Utilities' and 'Battery'. If the battery level falls below 20%, consider replacing the batteries to avoid the monitor turning off mid-workout; this is especially likely during the rest periods of an interval workout. PM5 users will know when the battery is low, as the monitor's backlight will turn off to conserve power.

ADDITIONAL HELP WITH INDOOR ROWING

If you are seeking additional guidance with indoor rowing, visit: cattrenthampersonaltraining.com to learn more about my coaching services.

As a rowing coach, my services include technical coaching to improve your rowing technique and boost your efficiency on the rowing machine. In addition, I offer various indoor rowing programmes and a personalised service providing customised feedback, pacing targets, and pacing strategies.

If you want to enhance your rowing proficiency and achieve your fitness goals, I can assist you in taking your performance from good to exceptional. Please don't hesitate to contact me for more information; I would love to help you on your rowing journey!

GLOSSARY OF TERMS

Aerobic energy system: The energy system that uses oxygen to generate energy for prolonged, low-intensity exercise, such as steady-state cardio.

Anaerobic energy system: The energy system that generates energy without oxygen for short, high-intensity exercise, such as high-intensity interval training (HIIT).

Average pace: The average speed at which a rower completes 500 meters, calculated over the entire duration of a workout; this is displayed as time per 500 meters.

Catch: The start of the stroke at the front end of the machine, where the rower is compressed with bent legs and vertical shins.

Cooldown: A low-intensity exercise after a workout aimed to help gradually lower the heart rate and help the body return to a resting state.

Concept2: A leading manufacturer of indoor rowing machines known for their high-quality and durable products, such as the Model D and Model E rowing machines.

Concept2 pace calculator: A tool provided by Concept2 to help rowers calculate various metrics, such as pace, time, and distance.

Current pace: The instantaneous speed at which a rower is rowing, displayed as time per 500 meters.

Damper setting: An adjustable feature on the rowing machine that controls airflow to the flywheel, affecting the feel and resistance of each stroke.

Drag factor: A numerical value representing the resistance experienced by the rower, calculated by the rowing machine based on the damper setting and other factors.

Drive Phase: The active part of the stroke where the rower pushes with their legs, engages the core, and pulls with the arms to generate power.

Drive length: The distance the rower travels during the drive phase of the stroke, which can be used to gauge efficiency and technique.

ErgData: An app which will provide additional information to the performance monitor and automatically synchronise workouts to your Concept2 online logbook.

Ergometer (erg): A device used to measure the work done during exercise. In indoor rowing, the term often refers to the rowing machine itself.

Even splits: A pacing strategy where a rower maintains a consistent pace throughout a workout, resulting in equal splits.

Finish: The end of the drive phase, where the rower's legs are extended, the handle is pulled to the chest, and they are slightly leaned back.

Fly and Die: A race strategy whereby a rower will begin at an unsustainably fast pace, leading to fatigue and decreased performance as the race continues. This approach is generally not recommended due to its adverse effects on race results.

Flywheel: The central component of a Concept2 rowing machine, responsible for generating resistance as the user pulls the handle.

Free rate: No specified stroke rate.

Heart rate workout zones: Ranges of heart rate intensity that correspond to different types of exercise, such as aerobic or anaerobic training.

Heavyweight: A classification for rowers based on body weight. In indoor rowing, this is typically above 75 kg for men and above 61.5 kg for women.

High-intensity interval training (HIIT): A workout method alternating between short bursts of intense exercise and periods of recovery or low-intensity activity.

Indoor rowing: The sport or exercise of rowing on a stationary machine, typically in a gym or home setting.

Intervals: A workout structure involving alternating work and rest/recovery periods.

Just row: A mode on the Concept2 performance monitor allowing the user to row without preset workout parameters or targets.

Lactic acid: A molecule produced by muscle cells during intense physical activity when insufficient oxygen is available to meet the cells' energy needs. It can cause fatigue, soreness, and a burning sensation in muscles.

Lightweight: A classification for rowers based on body weight; in indoor rowing, this is typically below 75 kg for men and below 61.5 kg for women.

Mesh outlet perf: This is the perforated metal part of the flywheel cage that wraps around the circumference of the flywheel.

Negative splits: A pacing strategy in which rowers gradually increase their speed throughout a workout, resulting in faster split times as the workout progresses.

Positive splits: A pacing strategy in which rowers gradually decrease their speed throughout a workout, resulting in slower split times as the workout progresses.

Predicted finish score: An estimate of the final time or distance a rower will achieve in a workout, calculated based on their current performance metrics.

Rate (r): A term used to represent strokes per minute, often abbreviated as "r." For example, 20 strokes per minute may be written as "r20" and verbally referred to as "rate 20."

Recovery: The passive part of the stroke where the rower returns to the catch position by extending the arms, hinging at the hips, and bending the knees.

Rollover meters: The distance rowed during rest periods or outside the designated work intervals in a workout. This measurement represents the additional meters achieved beyond the primary focus of the exercise session.

Sequencing: The proper order of movements in indoor rowing; these are crucial for efficient and powerful strokes.

Splits: A versatile term that can refer to various aspects of a rowing workout. 1). Current pace. 2). Overall pace: the average speed throughout the entire workout. 3). Individual workout sections: the specific segments of a workout as seen on the summary screen after completing the workout. Splits are typically expressed in time per 500 meters.

Steady-state cardio: A form of aerobic exercise performed at a constant, moderate intensity for an extended period, often used to improve endurance and cardiovascular fitness.

Stroke: A complete cycle of movement in indoor rowing, comprising the catch, drive, finish, and recovery phases.

Stroke rate: The number of strokes a rower takes per minute.

Summary: A post-workout report generated by the performance monitor provides an overview of the workout data, such as total time, distance, and average pace.

Technique: The proper execution of movements and body positions in indoor rowing. This is essential for efficient and injury-free performance.

Verification codes: Unique alphanumeric codes generated by the Concept2 performance monitor after a workout are used to validate and submit results for online rankings or competitions.

Warmup: A low-to-moderate intensity exercise performed before a workout, designed to increase heart rate, blood flow, and muscle temperature to prepare the body for more intense activity.

Made in the USA
Coppell, TX
12 December 2024

42406917R00040